HOLES

page 2

page 14

Diana Bentley

**Story illustrated by
Pet Gotohda**

D1471013

Heinemann

In this story

 Bones

 The master

 Wag

Introduce these tricky words and help the reader when they come across them later!

Tricky words

- paper
- door
- pulled

Story starter

Bones is a big dog. Wag is a small dog. Bones is a very good dog but Wag is always getting into trouble. One day, Bones saw the newspaper in the letter box in the door.

The Newspaper

Bones saw the paper in the door.

Bones ran to the door to get the paper.

20

Bones pulled the paper out of
the door.

Bones took the paper to his master.

The master took the paper.

"Good dog, Bones," said his master.

The master gave Bones a bone.

Wag saw the paper in the door.

Wag ran to the door to get the paper.

Wag pulled and pulled at the paper.

Wag took the paper
to his master.

"Bad dog, Wag!" said his master.

Quiz

Text Detective

- What did Wag do wrong?
- Do you feel sorry for Wag?

Word Detective

- **Phonic Focus:** Final phonemes
  Page 6: Find a word ending with the phoneme 'k'.
- Page 4: Find a word that rhymes with 'can'.
- Page 10: Find the word 'pulled' twice.

Super Speller

Read these words:

bad   ran

Now try to spell them!

HA! **HA! HA!**

 Q Why have you got holes in your trousers?

A I wouldn't be able to get my legs into them otherwise!

13

Find out about

- All sorts of holes

Tricky words

- guess
- whale
- blow-hole
- jumper

Introduce these tricky words and help the reader when they come across them later!

Text starter

There are lots of different sorts of holes. You might think that holes are bad, but not all holes are bad. Can you guess which holes are good?

Good Holes and Bad Holes

There are lots of holes.

Some holes are good.

Guess what this hole is.

This hole is on a whale.
It is a blow-hole.

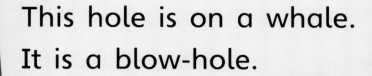

A whale breathes through its blow-hole.

It is a good hole.

Some holes are not good.

Guess what this hole is.

This hole is in a jumper.

It is not a good hole.

Some holes are small.

Guess what this hole is.

This hole is in a mint.

Is it a good hole?

Some holes are big.

Some holes are very big.

This is the biggest hole in the world.

Quiz

Text Detective

- Are all the holes in this book good holes?
- Have you ever made a hole in something?

Word Detective

- **Phonic Focus:** Final phonemes
  Page 16: Find a word ending with the phoneme 'd'.
- Page 20: Find a word meaning 'little'.
- Page 20: Find a word that rhymes with 'mess'.

Super Speller

Read these words:

not   big

Now try to spell them!

HA! HA! HA!

 What has no beginning, no end, and nothing in the middle?

ᗄ A polo mint.